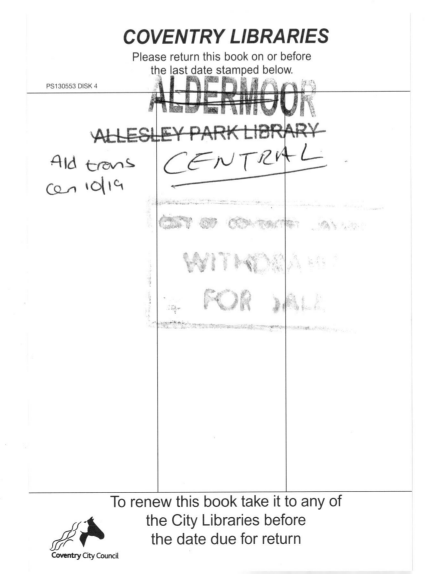

ATLAS OF WORLD FAITHS

HINDUISM

Rasamandala Das

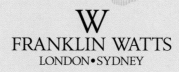

FRANKLIN WATTS
LONDON·SYDNEY

First published in 2007 by Franklin Watts

© 2007 Arcturus Publishing Limited

Franklin Watts
338 Euston Road
London NW1 3BH

Franklin Watts Australia
Level 17/207 Kent St, Sydney, NSW 2000

Produced by Arcturus Publishing Limited,
26/27 Bickels Yard, 151–153 Bermondsey Street,
London SE1 3HA

Series concept: Alex Woolf
Editor and picture researcher: Alex Woolf
Designer: Simon Borrough
Cartography: Encompass Graphics
Consultant: Douglas G Heming

Picture credits:
Art Archive: 17t (Musée Guimet Paris/Dagli Orti).
Bhaktivedanta Book Trust International: 5, 6, 26, 38.
Corbis: 9 (Diego Lezama Orezzoli), cover and 15 (Jayanta
Shaw/Reuters), 17b (David Cumming/Eye Ubiquitous),
19 (Anders Ryman), 24 (Stapleton Collection), 28
(Bettmann), 31 (Bob Krist), 33 (Hulton-Deutsch
Collection), 34 (David Cumming/Eye Ubiquitous), 37
(David Bebber/Reuters), 41 (Sherwin Castro/Reuters).
Goloka Books: 10.
Radha Mohan: 13.
Rasamandala Das: 20.
Vishnumaya Devi Dasi: 23.

A CIP catalogue record for this book is available from the
British Library.

Dewey Decimal Classification Number: 294.5

ISBN: 978 0 7496 6978 2

Printed in China

Franklin Watts is a division of Hachette Children's Books.

CONTENTS

CHAPTER 1:
THE ROOTS OF
HINDUISM
(c. 3000–1500 BCE)

induism is perhaps the oldest living religion in the world today. It is difficult to say exactly how it started. Unlike most other faiths, it has no single founder, no one scripture, and no commonly agreed set of teachings. Throughout its long history, there have been many leaders, teaching different philosophies and writing thousands of holy books. Hinduism, therefore, is often called 'a family of religions', or 'a way of life'. Its roots are in ancient India, going back more than 4,000 years. Today, however, large numbers of Hindus live outside India. Many are not even of Indian descent, but have adopted the teachings and practice of Hinduism. So, even though Hinduism is connected to India, it is also much broader.

Ancient Indian wisdom

Many followers say that their tradition is derived from sacred texts called the Vedas. *Veda*, an ancient Sanskrit word, simply means 'knowledge'. Hinduism does not limit its idea of truth to a single faith or creed but encourages flexibility of thought. To Hindus, being a good person is more important than what you believe. Despite this, most Hindus share certain key beliefs, such as the existence of the eternal soul which continuously reincarnates (passes from one body to another).

These ancient teachings were first passed on by word of mouth. According to tradition, they were first written down about 5,000 years ago. Many scholars believe the texts to be much younger, and date the compilation of the first book, the Rig Veda, to around 1000 BCE.

The eternal religion

The Vedas do not mention the term *Hinduism*. They talk of *dharma*, often translated as 'religious duty'. More precisely, it means 'duties that

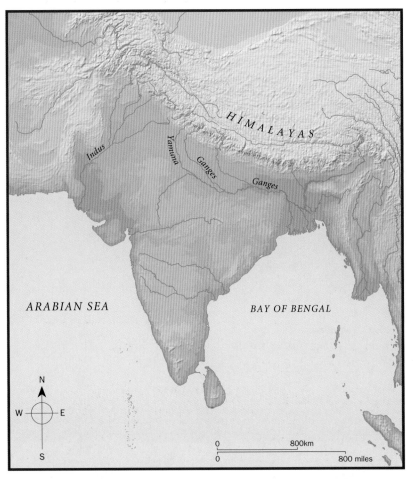

This map shows the geographical features of the Indian peninsula, often called the Indian subcontinent. It is bounded to the north by the Himalayas, to the west by the Arabian Sea and to the east by the Bay of Bengal. It is most vulnerable to attack through its north-west frontier.

A painting of the spiritual and material worlds. Hindus believe that the spiritual realm is eternal. For them, even this material world goes on forever, in an endless cycle of creation, destruction and re-creation.

sustain us according to who we are'. There are two main types of *dharma*:

1. Sanatana Dharma: actions based on the eternal relationship between the *atman* (soul) and God.

2. Varnashrama Dharma: duties according to the specific body we have, determined according to four *varnas* (social classes) and four *ashramas* (stages of life).

Many Hindus prefer to call their tradition Sanatana Dharma – the eternal religion.

The creation of the material world

Hindu books, such as the Rig Veda, describe an eternal world made of Brahman (spirit). They also discuss the repeated creation and destruction of this material world. Even after the present universe is destroyed, it is re-created as part of an everlasting cycle.

According to the Vedas, the Earth is only one of many planets, which exist both in different locations and on different dimensions. Although India is but one place on planet Earth, Hindus consider it special – a sacred land where many saints and avatars (incarnations of God) have lived.

PRAYER FROM THE RIG VEDA

Om. Oh Lord, the past, present and future universes are exhibitions of your powers, but You are greater still. The material [physical] creation is only one quarter of the entire cosmos [universe]. The eternal spiritual sky is much larger, making up the remaining three-quarters.

Rig Veda, Chapter 10, Hymn 190

Krishna and Arjuna blow their conch shells prior to the great Battle of Kurukshetra. Thirty-six years later, Krishna's departure from the world marked the start of the current age, the Kali yuga (age of iron).

Traditional accounts of history

Hinduism's early history is complex and there are many different accounts of it. There are three main reasons for this. Firstly, Hinduism is not a single religion, but includes many distinct branches. Secondly, there are differences of opinion between Hindus and Western researchers. Thirdly, Hinduism has no definite starting point. It goes back at least 4,000 or 5,000 years and maybe much further. To study Hinduism thoroughly, it is important to understand its views on time and its long history.

Hindus believe that since the creation of this universe, time has moved through cycles of four ages, which continuously repeat themselves like the four seasons. Apparently, during the first, golden age, people were virtuous and religious. Good qualities decreased through the silver and copper ages until we reached the present materialistic age, called the Kali yuga, the age of iron. *Kali yuga* literally means 'the age of quarrel'.

The two Hindu epics (long poems) give some information on Indian history, though some people consider them fictional rather than historical. The first, the Ramayana, tells the famous story of Rama and Sita, which may have happened as far back as the silver age. The second is called the Mahabharata, meaning 'the history of greater India'.

The Mahabharata happened at the very end of the last (copper) age, and relates the story of five princes called the Pandavas. They were sons of King Pandu and descendants of King Bharat, after whom India is named 'Bharatavarsha' (the land of Bharat), or simply 'Bharat'.

KEY HINDU IDEAS FOUND IN THE BHAGAVAD GITA

atman – the real, eternal self, which is neither the mind nor the body

Brahman – eternal spirit, different from temporary matter (*prakriti*)

samsara – the cycle of repeated birth and death (through reincarnation)

karma – the law of action and reaction: good actions bring a good next life, and vice-versa

moksha – liberation from *samsara* and the suffering it brings

God – perceived in three places: everywhere (as the world soul); in the heart (in humans, as conscience); and beyond the world (as the Supreme Person)

dharma – religious duty; duty in agreement with the timeless laws of God and nature

The Pandavas' cousins, known as the Kauravas, tried to usurp the throne of the vast Indian empire. After much intrigue, and requests for a peaceful settlement, the Kauravas refused to give up any of the land they had illegally occupied. To support the Pandavas, or to oppose them, kings from all over the known world prepared for battle on the planes of Kurukshetra, north of present-day New Delhi.

Just prior to the great battle, Lord Krishna – one of the most important Hindu deities – spoke the Bhagavad Gita (now a key Hindu text) to Arjuna, one of the five Pandavas. Arjuna, though a great warrior, was depressed at the prospect of fighting against his own cousins. Krishna explained all the important Vedic concepts, starting with the idea that the true self (*atman*) is not the body. Upon hearing the Bhagavad Gita, Arjuna regained his composure and resolved to fight. He and his brothers emerged victorious, securing the throne of the Indian Empire. Thirty-six years later, Krishna departed the world, marking the start of the present age.

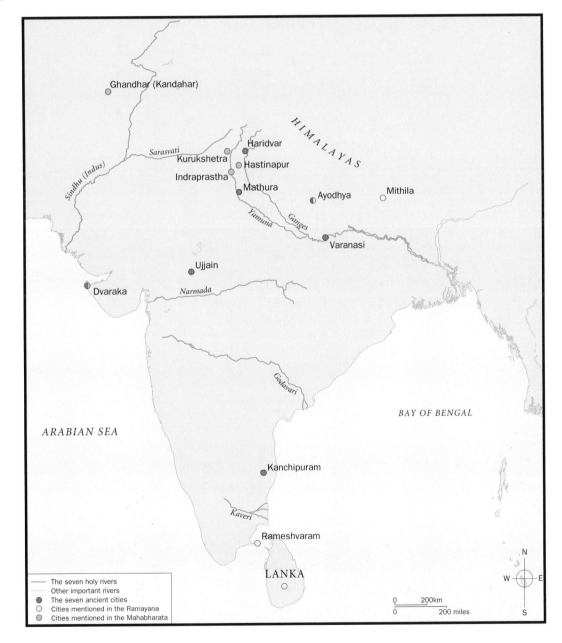

This map shows India's seven holy rivers, the seven ancient cities and other sites mentioned in the two Hindu epics, the Ramayana and the Mahabharata.

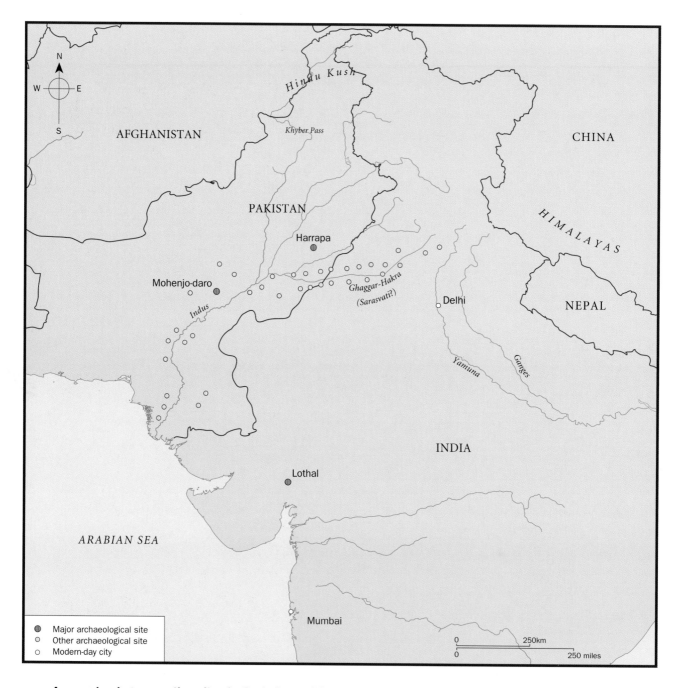

A map showing excavation sites in the Indus and Sarasvati valleys. The course of the legendary River Sarasvati is uncertain, but it may correspond to the Ghaggar-Hakra River (as shown here).

The Aryan invasion theory

When Europeans first arrived in India, they knew little of the origins of Hinduism. They found very few historical records. They certainly studied religious accounts of history, but often considered them mythological, and therefore unreliable. They noted, however, that the Hindu scriptures talked of 'Aryans'. The Sanskrit word *Aryan* literally means 'noble people', but academics suggested that it referred to a distinct race of people. Max Muller, the German linguist, proposed that the Aryans came from outside India, from the west, bringing with them the ancient language of Sanskrit and the beginnings of Hinduism as we know it today.

However, little was known of the Aryan people. Then, in the 1920s, archaeologists unearthed the remains of two walled cites, Mohenjo-Daro and

Harappa (both in present-day Pakistan). There was evidence of detailed town planning, with orderly streets and sophisticated drainage systems. The inhabitants even developed what appears to be a form of writing, depicted on various seals found throughout the sites. One seal portrays a figure that resembles Lord Shiva, now an important Hindu deity. To date, experts have been unable to decipher the script. However, scholars were amazed at how civilized the inhabitants had been. Even more surprisingly, they appeared to have lived well before the Aryans. This challenged the theory that the Aryans were the most advanced race of their time.

Ruins at Mohenjo-Daro in present-day Pakistan. This site, and the one at Harappa, were excavated in the 1920s.

Revised theories Rather than rejecting the original invasion theory, scholars revised it. They now proposed that the Aryan invaders had conquered and destroyed the cities of the much-older Indus valley civilization. Subsequently, Aryan beliefs and practices blended with those of the local peoples, including the dark-skinned Dravidians (from the south), giving rise to what we now call Hinduism.

More recent finds of artefacts indicate that the Indus valley civilization was more widespread than first imagined and support the existence of the legendary River Sarasvati (now dried up). This suggested that the river was not a myth, as previously thought, and that Hindu accounts of history could be taken more seriously. Hindus texts, however, do not mention an Aryan invasion.

Controversial debates Scholars now more seriously consider the possibility that Hinduism developed within India, and not beyond it. Several Hindu thinkers, and a few Western scholars, have extended these ideas to claim that India is the 'cradle of civilization', and not Europe or Central Asia, as previously thought. Naturally, some Indian nationalists favour this idea! The result is that contemporary scholars have started to debate previous theories and often accept earlier dates, more in line with Hindu tradition. However, it is unlikely that anyone will conclusively establish the origins of Hinduism.

EUROPEAN WORDS FROM SANSKRIT

Sanskrit experts have noted how many European words seem to come from Sanskrit. Some suggest that words appear similar because both Sanskrit and the European tongues developed from a common 'Indo-European' language. In relation to English, the following Sanskrit words illustrate the similarities between the two languages:

Mata – mother
Pita (father) - paternal
Duhita – daughter
Agni (god of fire) – ignite
Sama – same
Sarpa – serpent

CHAPTER 2:
THE TEACHINGS ARE WRITTEN DOWN
(1500 BCE–500 CE)

India's distant past is uncertain. Nonetheless, we know that its ancient wisdom was first passed down by word of mouth, and later written down. Tradition states that a sage called Vyasa recorded the teachings on palm leaves about 5,000 years ago. Scholars claim that the first books, the four Vedas, were composed more recently, around 1000 BCE. This period, from about 1500 to 500 BCE, is therefore known as 'the Vedic age'. *Vedic* means 'related to the Vedas'.

Although there are only four main Vedas, there are hundreds of later texts based upon them. All these writings fall into one of two broad categories, called the *shruti* and the *smriti*. Together, they are called 'the Vedic literature'.

The Vedas included hymns and chants for use in rituals, and sections on philosophy.

The four main books are:
- The Rig Veda – hymns to various deities
- The Yajur Veda – a handbook for priests to use during *yajna* (sacrifices)
- The Sama Veda – chants and melodies
- The Artharva Veda – more hymns and mantras

The main practice during the Vedic age was the performance of elaborate *yajnas*. The aim was to join the ancestors in heaven after death. The most popular *yajna* was the *havan* (sacred fire ceremony), in which priests tossed grains into the flames as an offering to various deities.

The *havan* was accompanied by the chanting of mantras. A mantra is a string of sacred syllables. For a sacrifice to be successful, it was essential that the mantras were pronounced correctly.

A painting of a *havan*, attended largely by members of the royal and priestly *varnas* (social classes).

THE MAIN VEDIC (HINDU) TEXTS

Shruti – 'that which is heard'
- The Vedas (prayers and philosophy)
- The Upanishads (philosophy)

Smriti – 'that which is remembered'
- The Vedanta Sutra (aphorisms)
- The Puranas (stories and histories)
- The Epics: (1) The Ramayana
                      (2) The Mahabharata
- The Bhagavad Gita (philosophy)
- The Dharma Shastra (moral codes)

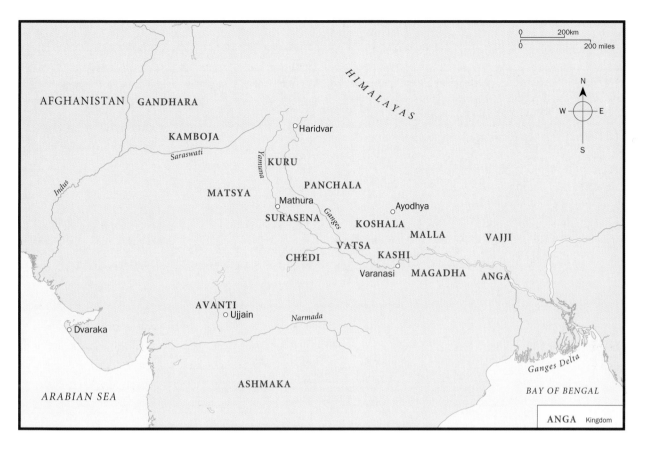

The 16 ancient kingdoms stretched from Afghanistan in the west to the Ganges Delta in the east. Most were situated either around the Doab, the fertile area between the Ganges and the Yamuna, or further down the Ganges after the joining of the two rivers at Prayag.

The deities The main deities were connected to nature, perhaps because the Vedas emphasized the need to live in harmony with the rhythms of nature, called *rita*. The chief deity was Indra, the rain god, also called 'the king of heaven'. Agni was also important, for he presided over the sacred fire into which all offerings were made.

The main Vedic deities were:
- Indra – god of rain
- Agni – god of fire
- Varuna – god of the waters
- Vayu – the wind god
- Rudra – god of the storms
- Usha – goddess of dawn
- Sarasvati – a river goddess
- Kuvera – god of wealth
- Soma – the moon god
- Surya – the sun god

Books of philosophy Gradually the importance of ritual diminished as priority was given to philosophical thought. Ideas were gleaned from specific sections of the Vedas, called the Upanishads, and were later summarized in an anthology (collection) of aphorisms (profound sayings), now called the 'Vedanta Sutra', or the 'Brahma Sutra'.

Hindu kingdoms The scholars who taught from these sacred books belonged to the priestly *varna* (class) and were dedicated to spiritual life. They did not receive wages but were dependent upon the financial support of pious Hindu kings, who were members of the warrior *varna*. Since ancient times, the warrior and priestly *varnas* had co-operated to protect and educate the general citizens. By 600 BCE, 16 Hindu kingdoms stretched across the Indian plains, from modern-day Afghanistan to beyond the Ganges delta.

The Mauryan Empire (c. 321–184 BCE)

Towards the end of the Vedic period, the Magadha kingdom, as mentioned in the Mahabharata, rose to power. From 350 BCE, this eastern tract of land (now comprising the states of Bengal and Bihar) was ruled by the Nanda Dynasty. In 326, Alexander the Great of Macedonia (a kingdom in Greece) conquered the north-western part of India, defeating King Porus of the Punjab and alarming other Hindu kings. However, upon approaching the formidable Magadha kingdom, Alexander's exhausted army mutinied, turned south towards the coast, and finally sailed westwards away from India.

Taking advantage of Alexander's retreat, Chandragupta defeated the Nandas and ascended the throne of Magadha. He repelled an invasion by the remaining Greek forces headed by Seleucus, a former general in Alexander's army. Establishing a long-term friendship with the Greeks, Chandragupta extended his territory to establish the Mauryan Empire, the most powerful empire of ancient India. One of Chandragupta's successors, Ashoka (273–232 BCE), further extended Mauryan territory. Ashoka later converted to Buddhism, ushering in a period of peace. He spread Buddhist ideals throughout India and beyond, even into Mediterranean Europe.

Writings

During the Mauryan period, many important texts were compiled. Chandragupta's prime minister and close advisor, Chanakya, wrote the Artha Shastra, a work that deals with war, economics and political philosophy. He also compiled the Niti Shastra, a collection of proverbs still widely read today. Many of his teachings were drawn from earlier, oral texts, such as the Manu Smriti (the laws of mankind). The Manu Smriti was also written down around this time, forming

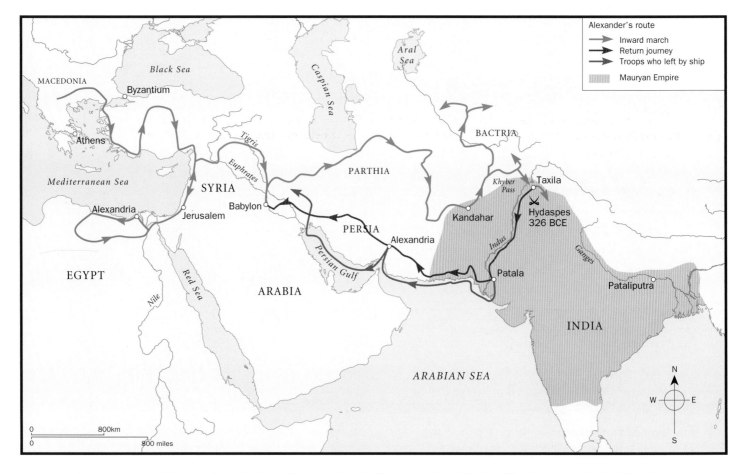

A map showing Alexander's route from Macedonia to India, where he defeated King Porus at the Battle of Hydaspes. Soon afterwards, Alexander's army mutinied and withdrew from the subcontinent, allowing King Chandragupta to found the Mauryan Empire.

Temple *murtis* of Sita and Rama, accompanied by Rama's brother Lakshmana (left) and the monkey warrior Hanuman (kneeling). Between 500 BCE and 500 CE, temple *puja* took over from *yajna* (sacrifice) as the main method of worship.

a part of the Vedic canon called the Dharma Shastra (moral codes).

Around this time, the two Hindu epics were written down: the Ramayana, recorded by Valmiki, and the Mahabharata by Vyasa. These works explored the ideal of performing one's *dharma* (religious duty), and especially the key role played by chivalrous kings and their learned advisers, the *brahmins* (priests).

Puja From 500 BCE onwards, the complex rituals and sacrifices, such as the *havan*, were largely superseded by *puja*, the worship of sacred statues called *murtis* (see panel). At the same time, the focus of worship moved from Indra and the other Vedic gods, to three main deities: Vishnu, Shiva and Shakti (the goddess, also called Devi). Later, during the Gupta period, many magnificent temples were specifically dedicated to these principal deities.

THE *MURTI*

The *murti* (sacred statue) remains an essential feature of Hindu worship. The temple *murtis* are treated with respect, as if they are great kings and queens. Each day, the priests bathe and dress the deities, garland them with flowers and offer vegetarian food and other items of worship. Hindu families often worship small *murtis* at their home shrine. Sacred texts explain that God – invisible to most of us – appears through the *murti* to accept the worshipper's devotion. However, for God to be present, these practices must be performed according to strict rules, requiring cleanliness, punctuality and devotion.

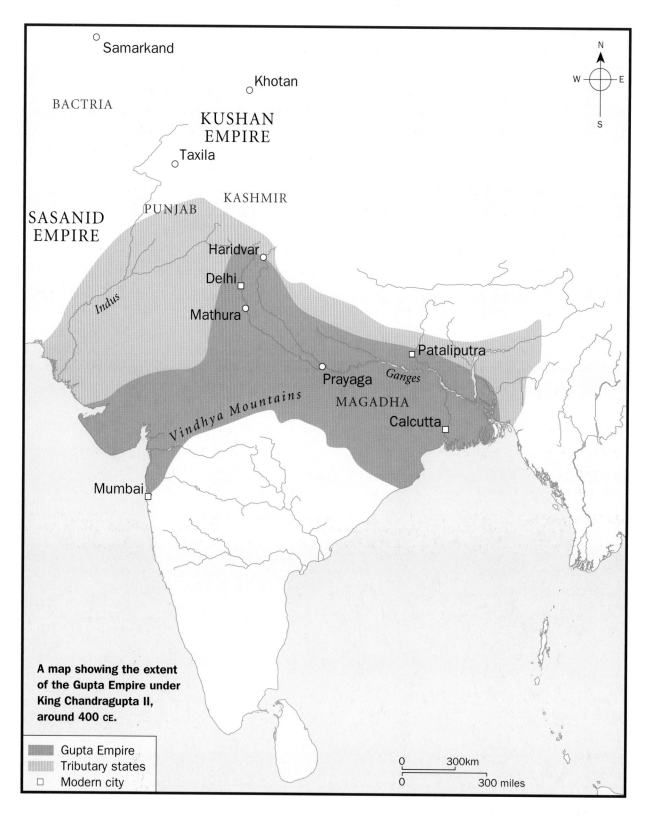

A map showing the extent of the Gupta Empire under King Chandragupta II, around 400 CE.

- ◼ Gupta Empire
- ▥ Tributary states
- □ Modern city

The Gupta dynasty The reign of Ashoka was followed by a succession of weaker kings and the eventual collapse of the Mauryan Empire. Invaders known as the Kushans penetrated the north-west frontier, bringing a period of relative instability to north India. The Gupta dynasty (320–550 CE) expelled the Kushans and for two centuries ruled all land north of the Vindhya Mountains. The Gupta Empire, though not as vast as the Mauryan before it, left a deep cultural impression on India. Much historical evidence has been derived from coins, monuments and inscriptions. Travellers wrote of fine cities, well-equipped hospitals, thriving universities and a content, prosperous people. For Hinduism, it was a time of cultural and economic expansion.

Gupta arts and religion

The Gupta period is now considered a golden age of Hinduism, marked by considerable achievement in art, music, literature, philosophy and architecture. These were largely forms of religious expression. For example, the first dances were not just entertainment, but were performed in temples for the pleasure of the deities. With the increasing popularity of *puja*, many impressive temples were constructed. There is also evidence that Hindu architecture extended deep into South-East Asia, reaching countries such as Cambodia, where the temples in Angkor Wat were dedicated to Vishnu and Shiva. Within the Gupta Empire, society was divided into different *varnas* (classes), according to Hindu teachings.

With the rise of temple worship, three main traditions emerged, focusing their respective worship on Vishnu, Shiva and Shakti. At the same time, the idea of the Trimurti (three main deities) developed. Brahma was considered responsible for creation; Vishnu became 'the sustainer and protector'; and the role of destroyer was given to Shiva (previously known as Rudra).

Shiva's wife is Shakti, also called Devi, Durga or Parvati. Shaktas (followers of Shakti) also venerate the other two wives of the Trimurti – Lakshmi (wife of Vishnu and goddess of fortune) and Sarasvati (wife of Brahma and goddess of learning).

The Puranas

During the Gupta period, the Puranas, or 'ancient stories', were written down. There were 18 main Puranas, dedicated to Brahma, Vishnu and Shiva, but with some references to Shakti. The most famous are those describing the activities of Krishna, a form of Vishnu. Krishna is celebrated for his mischievous activities as a child and youth in the village of Vrindavana, and especially for stealing butter and feeding it to the monkeys.

Another popular book, the Devi Bhagavata Purana, tells the story of the goddess Durga. She slayed a demon who took the form of a buffalo. Durga easily defeated him, surpassing the might of all the gods combined.

THE GREAT TRADITIONS

The three main traditions that emerged during the Gupta period were:

- **Vaishnavas** – who worship Vishnu
- **Shaivas** – who worship Shiva
- **Shaktas** – who worship Shakti (Devi)

Later on, around the ninth century CE, another tradition developed. Their followers, called Smartas, worship five deities; Vishnu, Shiva, Devi, Surya (the Sun god) and Ganesh (the deity with an elephant's head).

Brahma, though one of the Trimurti, is hardly worshipped at all, except in one town in India (Pushkar in Rajasthan) and in some parts of South-East Asia.

Indian dancers perform a dance retelling the story of Durga, a fierce form of the goddess Shakti. Durga has ten arms, wielding various weapons.

The Gupta Empire collapsed around 550 CE, largely due to military pressure from the Hunas, or 'White Huns', based in Afghanistan. For a brief period between 535 and 700, the Harsha Empire, centred around Kanauj on the River Ganges, united much of north India and helped stave off the raiding Hunas. King Harsha (ruled 606–647) supported Buddhism, and his kingdom was visited by Buddhist pilgrims such as Hsuan Tsang, the Chinese traveller and writer. Harsha was defeated by the Chalukyas, members of a warrior dynasty who briefly expanded their empire to encompass central India.

The Chola Empire (850–1279)

With the fragmentation of the Harsha Empire in 700, and the brief rise of the Chalukyas, power in India shifted southwards. The Chola dynasty, which had existed since the first century CE, gradually overcame the Chalukyas and other southern powers, such as the

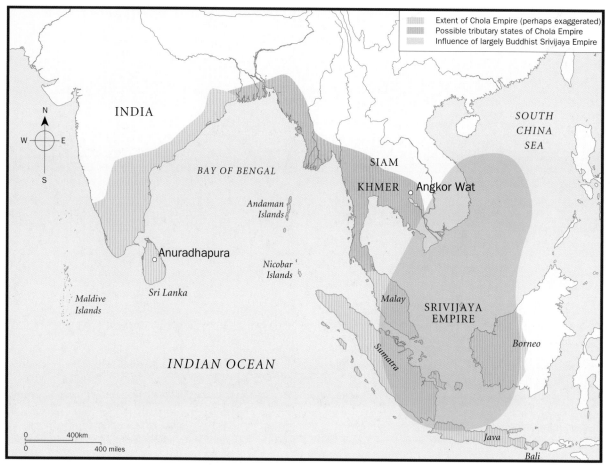

A map showing the extent of Chola influence in South-East Asia. The major temples at Angkor Wat in modern Cambodia were built between the 9th and 14th centuries, during the height of Chola power.

A statue of Nataraja from south India

practices intertwined with Buddhist and native traditions. This mixed culture still exists in many parts of Indochina and Indonesia, as evident in the continuing use of long Sanskrit names.

Pandhyas and Pallavas. At the height of their power, between the ninth and thirteenth centuries, the Cholas attacked the Buddhist rulers of Bengal, the powerful Pala Dynasty. The Cholas were the first Indian rulers to maintain a fleet in order to extend their territory beyond the Indian peninsula.

The Cholas were devotees of Shiva, but also supported the other main traditions, Vaishnavism and Shaktism. They built many impressive temples, particularly in Thanvajur and in their capital city, Chidambaram. These temples featured large *gopurams*, towering gateways decorated with ornate carvings of the various gods and goddesses. Shiva remained the most popular deity, particularly in his form as Nataraja, the 'king of dancers'.

Hinduism in South-East Asia

Hinduism may have reached places such as Cambodia as early as the first century CE. With the aid of its fleet, the Chola Empire further colonized countries to the south and south-east, including the Maldive Islands, Sri Lanka and lands belonging to the largely Buddhist Srivijaya Empire in Indonesia (which included Malaya, Java and Sumatra). Chola armies exacted tribute (taxes) from rulers on the Indochina peninsula, especially from Siam (present-day Thailand) and the Khmer kingdom of Cambodia.

Around this time, Hinduism reached the island of Bali, where it remains the principal religion. Throughout South-East Asia, Hindu beliefs and

THE ROLE OF THE TEMPLE

Within Hinduism, the temple (*mandir*) is considered the home of God, or of the specific deity whose image stands in the central shrine. The main act of worship, called *arti*, is performed up to six or seven times each day. During this welcoming ceremony, the priest offers the deities pleasing items such as incense, water, flowers and a lamp.

In the west, temples also serve as community centres. Some recent purpose-built complexes have been built in modern architectural style, but others conform to traditional designs, usually drawn from one of the two main styles, northern and southern. Northern temples feature a central shrine, a main spire (and often other smaller spires) and rounded arches. Southern temples are often situated in large complexes and are surrounded by several concentric walls. The central shrine is reached by entering towering *gopurams* (gateways), each profusely decorated with carvings of gods and goddesses.

An exterior view of the Brihadisvara Temple at Thanvajur.

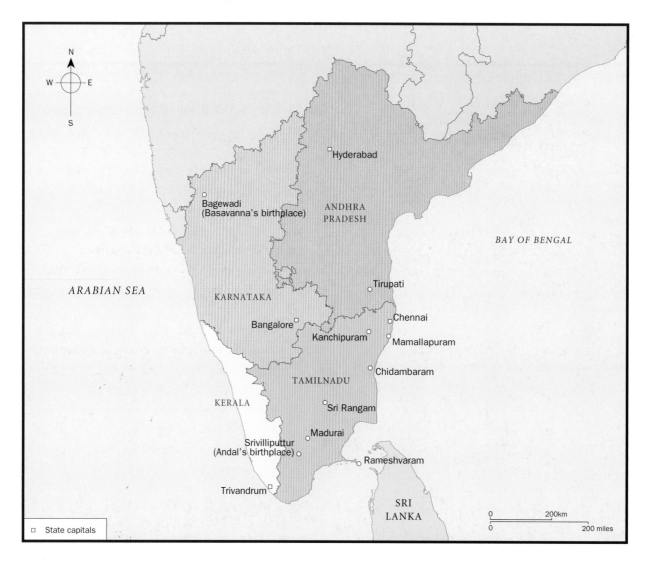

A map of the four states in southern India, showing places connected to the poet-saints.

The poet-saints of south India

Between the sixth and tenth centuries, poet-saints in southern India helped Hinduism move away from the strict, *brahmin*-controlled ritual of the Vedic times. Their focus on a personal God laid the foundations for modern Hinduism. Writing in the Tamil tongue, the poet-saints established its importance as a sacred language, much like Sanskrit in the north.

Among the poet-saints were the 63 Nayanars. They were fervent devotees of Shiva, and largely unconcerned with philosophical study. They dedicated themselves to practical service, such as cleaning the temple premises, lighting the lamps, stringing flower garlands, feeding the devotees and performing other humble tasks around the temple. They regarded worship of Lord Shiva's devotees

to be paramount, even higher than the worship of Shiva himself. The Nayanars helped establish the important tradition now called Shaiva Siddhanta.

The Vaishnava (Vishnu-worshipping) equivalents of the Nayanars were the twelve Alvars. Most famous was the female saint, Andal, who as a young girl resolved to accept only Krishna as her husband. She was ritually married to the image of Krishna. According to legend, as the ceremony concluded, she miraculously disappeared into the *murti*. Andal's life and poetry are still celebrated during a festival that falls in December or January.

The poems of the twelve Alvars were compiled into the 4,000 verses of the 'Divya Prabhandham', which remains a core text in south India. It sings the praises of Vishnu in his form as the four-handed Narayan. It is still

FOUR GOALS AND FOUR PATHS

Hindu teachings list four goals for human life:

- *dharma* – performing religious duties
- *artha* – developing wealth and prosperity
- *kama* – enjoying pleasures of the senses in an ethical way
- *moksha* – gaining liberation from birth and death

There are four *margs* (paths) towards *moksha*, also called yogas, or 'ways of linking' to God. They are:

- *karma-yoga* – the path of selfless work
- *jnana-yoga* – the path of philosophy and wisdom
- *astanga-yoga* – the path of exercises and meditation
- *bhakti-yoga* – the path of devotional service, *bhakti* appears most popular today, though it is often mixed with practices from the other three yogas.

recited daily in the famous Shri Rangam Temple on the banks of the River Kaveri (one of India's seven sacred rivers).

Bhakti movements

The poet-saints came from all walks of life and cared little for the Hindu social structure, which by then had evolved into the hereditary caste system. By accepting disciples from all social classes, the saints challenged the authority of caste-conscious *brahmins* (priests).

The poet-saints gave rise to popular *bhakti* movements (movements of religious devotion) that later swept north to embrace all of India. One of the first *bhakti* movements was founded in the 12th century by a scholar called Basavanna. Members were called Lingayats, after the small lingam they always carried. The sacred lingam is a cylindrical black stone considered to represent Lord Shiva. The Lingayats believed in one God and rejected the Vedas, considering them to be polytheistic (encouraging a belief in many gods). They taught about the equality of all beings, and – unusually for the time – accepted women as gurus (religious teachers).

Devotional activities inside a temple in India. The women are praying and making offerings to a large lingam, the symbol of Shiva, while a priest reads from holy scripture.

A traditional painting of Adi Shankara.

Darshan literally means 'seeing'. The *darshans* are ways of seeing the truth from different perspectives. Each stresses different beliefs or practices:

1. **Vaisheshika** The theory that everything is made of atoms
2. **Nyaya** The practices of logic and philosophical debate
3. **Sankhya** A philosophy that divides the world into different elements
4. **Yoga** Physical exercises, breathing techniques and meditation
5. **Mimamsa** The practices of ritual, such as the *havan* and *puja*
6. **Vedanta** A philosophy concerned with the soul, God and matter.

Modern Hinduism favours Vedanta, but also draws on the other five *darshans*.

Scholars and philosophers

Around the time of the poet-saints, there lived several key thinkers, known as *acharyas*, who between them laid the foundations for modern Hindu thought. Each *acharya* started his own branch of philosophy. To spread their ideas, they each established a *sampradaya*, an unbroken line of teachers and students (who in turn become teachers). The *acharyas* reinforced the importance of the relationship between the guru (spiritual teacher) and the disciple. For them, knowledge was not merely gathering information but was based on developing character and deep understanding, through moral conduct and spiritual discipline.

Vedanta philosophy The *acharyas* taught versions of Vedanta philosophy. *Vedanta* means 'the conclusion of the Vedas', and is one of the six *darshans* ('orthodox' schools) in Hinduism (see panel). The *darshans* are not entirely distinct schools of thought, but represent different ways of viewing the same truth. Vedanta developed two main ideas about God: the first, that he is impersonal, the ever-present world soul; the second, that God is ultimately a person, living beyond this material world. Many traditions combine these two views.

Shankara Shankara (c. 780–812) was born in what is today the southern state of Kerala. According to legend, he renounced the world at the age of eight to become a *sannyasi* (wandering monk). He later accepted initiation from a spiritual teacher, who asked him to write commentaries on Vedanta philosophy.

At the time of Shankara, Hinduism had lost some of its appeal because of the widespread influence of Buddhism and Jainism. Hindus had accepted Buddha as an avatar (incarnation) of Vishnu. Nonetheless, many Hindus considered Buddhists and Jains unorthodox for their rejection of the Vedic texts. Shankara travelled throughout India, re-establishing the authority of the Vedic literature and defeating opposing arguments.

He started the *advaita* school of Vedanta, teaching that the soul and God are identical. He founded a fourth strand of Hinduism called the Smarta school, distinct from the already existing Vaishnava, Shaiva and Shakta

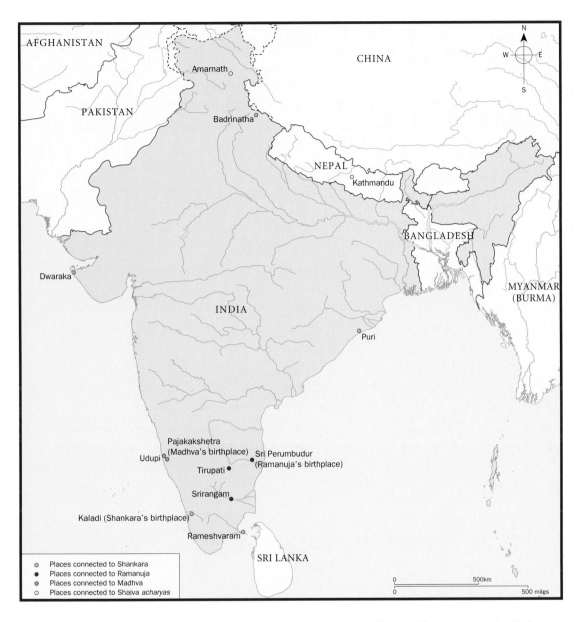

A map showing the cities and holy sites connected to the major Hindu philosophers and scholars.

traditions (see page 15). He also established monasteries in four places, representing the four cardinal directions – in the north, east, south and west of India.

Ramanuja and Madhva

Ramanuja (1017–1137) was the most important *acharya* amongst the Shri Vaishnava *sampradaya* of south India. He extended Shankara's doctrine: for Ramanuja, God not only exists everywhere as a formless energy (as Shankara taught), but is also a person with a spiritual body. Salvation is obtained largely through grace (God's favour), by which the soul (*atman*) enters Vishnu's abode to live forever in a spiritual form. Today, Tirupati and Shri Rangam in south India remain the main centres of Shri Vaishnavism.

More strongly than Ramanuja before him, Madhva (1238–1317) stressed the personal form of God (as Krishna) and the eternal distinction between God and the soul (*atman*). The headquarters of the Madhva tradition are in Udupi in the state of Karnataka.

Ramanuja and Madhva were both Vaishnavas. There were also several Shaiva (Shiva-worshipping) *acharyas*, such as Abhinavagupta, Srikantha and Bhojadeva, who taught their own philosophies.

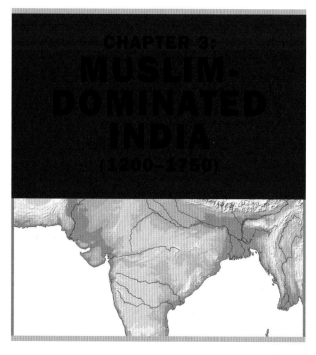

By the 11th century, while Hindu kingdoms flourished in the south, religious life was threatened in the north. The relatively new religion of Islam had first reached India through traders plying the Arabian Sea in the seventh century. In the eighth century, Iraqi Arabs occupied the north-western state of Sind. Steadily, Muslims from Turkey and Central Asia superseded Persia as the major power to the west of India.

Particularly brutal were the incursions of Mahmud of Ghazni (971–1030), the Afghan emperor. In raids against the northern states, he sacked temples, plundering gold, jewels and slaves. In 1025, he flattened the Shiva temple in Somnatha, slaughtering its residents. It is said that Mahmud personally hacked the gilded image to pieces and sent the stone fragments back to his capital, Ghazni, to be set in the steps of a new mosque.

Mahmud seized control of much of the north-west of India, including modern Pakistan and Indian Punjab. The period following his death in 1030 saw the gradual erosion of his empire, as Punjab was reclaimed by Hindu kings. To the west, power was seized by Turks and Afghans based in the city of Ghor. From there they continued to raid northern India.

The Delhi Sultanate

In 1192, Muhammad of Ghor defeated the Hindu king Pritviraj and overran the city of Delhi. Upon Muhammad's assassination in 1206, his successor, Qutb ud-Din, established the first Muslim kingdom in India. The Delhi Sultanate refers to various Muslim dynasties that ruled in India until 1526. A string of sultans subdued the whole of India, with the exception of Kashmir in the far north and the Hindu kingdom of Vijayanagar in the south.

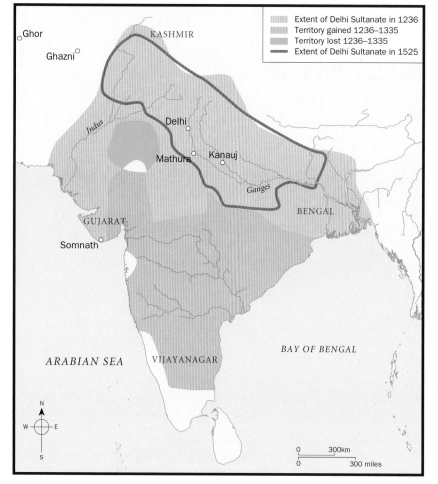

The rise and decline of the Delhi Sultanate from 1236 until 1525, the year before the Mughal invasion led by Babur.

The fall of Delhi in 1192 marked the beginning of over five centuries of Muslim rule in India. It was to have a significant effect on the way Hinduism developed. Islam was sometimes hostile towards Hinduism, especially the practice of image worship. The ancient tradition of Sanatana Dharma (as Hinduism used to be called), well known as inclusive and tolerant, was forced to redefine itself. The ancient Persians had first coined the term *Hindu* in the seventh century, referring to the people living on the far side of the River Indus. By the 1400s, the term had been adopted by those who practised the faith, to distinguish themselves from members of other religions.

The Hindu social system By the time the Muslims arrived, the ancient Indian system of four *varnas* had become hereditary (the modern caste system). Birth in a high family usually guaranteed a prestigious job, even for the unqualified. Those born in lower castes were forced into menial work, even if talented in other professions. Muslim rule created a governing elite, reinforcing class differences and bolstering the caste system.

Under many Muslim rulers, Hindus were required to pay special taxes. Sometimes they were forcibly converted to Islam. About a quarter of Hindus converted, mainly in the north-west and in Bengal.

Traditional *sannyasis* dressed in saffron robes and carrying staffs. The Hindu emphasis on personal spirituality helped many such practices to endure despite centuries of foreign rule and social change.

THE FOUR *VARNAS* AND THE CASTE SYSTEM

The Rig Veda describes four varnas (social classes):

- *brahmins* – priests and intellectuals
- *kshatriyas* – army, police and administrators
- *vaishyas* – traders and business community
- *sudras* – workers and labourers

Originally, a person was assigned to a *varna* according to their preference for a particular type of work. Later, the system became hereditary, and many sub-divisions (*jati*) were added. Today it is called the caste system.

Dating from the Mughal period, a painting of Krishna and his girlfriend, Radha. During Akbar's reign, Hindu art, music and architecture flourished, but much was later destroyed by the ruthless Aurangzeb.

The Mughal Empire

Due to fierce rivalry between different factions in government, the Delhi Sultanate gradually descended into civil war. In 1398, the capital, Delhi, was ruthlessly destroyed by Timur, a Muslim conqueror who claimed descent from the Mongol emperor, Genghis Khan. The Sultanate never fully recovered, and eventually, in 1526, Delhi fell to Babur, a Muslim descendent of Timur's from Central Asia. Babur subsequently established the Mughal dynasty, which ruled much of India for the following three centuries.

The Mughal Empire reached the peak of its glory (though not its greatest size) under Akbar, Babur's grandson. Born and raised in India, Akbar displayed a positive attitude towards all religions. He celebrated Hindu festivals and began a series of religious debates to which he invited not only Muslims but also Hindus, Sikhs and Christians. He also encouraged members of other faiths to enter his government. During his long reign (1542–1605), Akbar extended the kingdom and left many fine buildings and works of art. He is remembered as the greatest of the Mughal emperors.

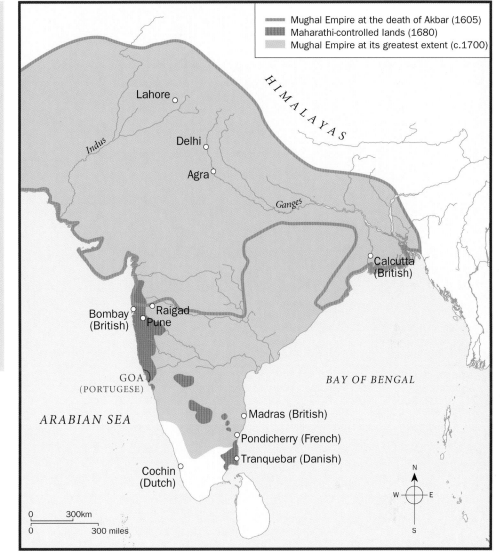

Mughal Empire at the death of Akbar (1605)
Maharathi-controlled lands (1680)
Mughal Empire at its greatest extent (c.1700)

The growth of the Mughal Empire from the death of Akbar in 1605 until 1700. By the end of the 17th century, European traders had established several important outposts, which threatened Mughal supremacy.

Akbar was succeeded by his son, Jahangir, and then his grandson, Shah Jahan (1592–1666), famed for building the Taj Mahal (in Agra) and the Red Fort (in Delhi). Shah Jahan's son, Aurangzeb, was tyrannical, slaying his brothers, imprisoning his father and proclaiming himself emperor. During his long reign (1668–1707), he discriminated against Hindus, imposing heavy taxes on them and defacing their temples and sacred images. Aurangzeb's religious policies contributed to Muslim–Hindu conflict in India, creating resentment that endures to modern times. Where Aurangzeb did excel was in expanding Mughal territory, especially in the south. Upon his death, the Mughal Empire was at its largest, but rapidly fell into a steep decline from which it never recovered.

New Hindu kingdom During Muslim rule, two new Hindu kingdoms arose. In the south, the fabulously wealthy Vijayanagar (City of Victory) resisted the military might of both the Delhi Sultanate and the Mughals until its final collapse in 1565. This marked the end of the south as a separate political region. However, a more formidable foe of the Mughals emerged on the west coast of India, in the mountainous Maharathi kingdom. The Maharathi king Shivaji (1630–1680) and his successors relentlessly harassed Aurangzeb, hastening the end of Mughal rule. Shivaji was a resistance fighter who exemplified the ancient Hindu ideal of a pious and chivalrous warrior. For many modern Hindus, he remains a symbol of the righteous struggle against intolerance and oppression.

Left: A painting of Chaitanya dancing. He opposed the hereditary caste system and emphasized the importance of developing love for a personal God.

Below: The main states and towns on the Indian peninsula that are still influenced today by four of the prominent *bhakti* saints and their respective teachings.

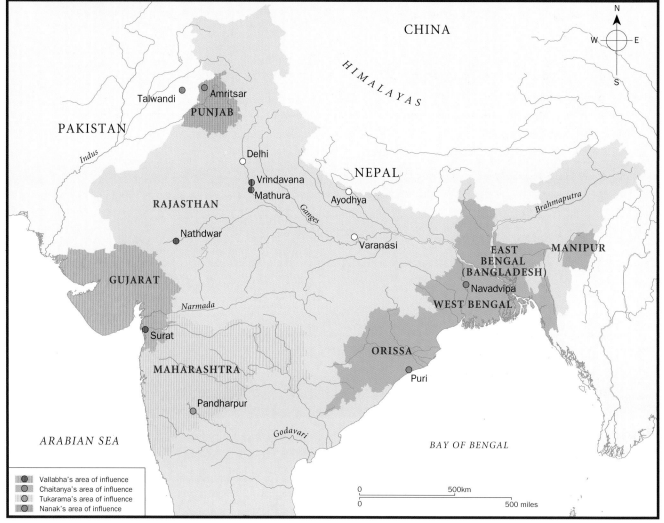

Bhakti sweeps India

The restraints of Mughal rule were compounded by the tight control exercised by Hindu priests. Many of these *brahmins* insisted on the strict observation of the hereditary caste system, which barred Hindus of lower birth from taking key roles in society, or fully participating in religious life. Ordinary Hindus felt marginalized. Leaders arose from amongst their ranks, stressing the spiritual equality of all, and the personal relationship everyone could develop with God. As a result, a wave of *bhakti*, or religious devotion, swept through India.

Bhakti saints

The leaders of this movement, known as *bhakti* saints, drew on the religious sentiments of the earlier south Indian poets, and also on Vedanta philosophy, especially as taught by Ramanuja and Madhva. Whereas the earlier poet-saints had worshipped Shiva and Vishnu, these largely northern traditions focused on Rama and Krishna, two principal avatars (incarnations) of Vishnu. Important saints at this time included:

- Chaitanya, who founded Bengali Vaishnavism
- Kabir, who taught that God is the same for all, whatever path they tread. His followers included Muslims, Sikhs and Hindus.
- Vallabha, who favoured worship of baby Krishna, a custom that is still popular with many Gujarati Hindus.
- Surdas, who was born blind but became an excellent musician and composed thousands of songs glorifying Lord Krishna.
- Tulsidas, who wrote a popular version of the Ramayana, known as Rama Carita Manas.
- Tukarama, who worshipped the famous deity of Vishnu, known as Vitthala, in Pandhapur (present-day Maharashtra, near Mumbai).
- Mirabai, who is perhaps the most famous female saint within Hinduism.

Music, mantra and dance

Many *bhakti* traditions popularized the chanting of mantras, either out loud to music or softly on prayer beads. The saints also composed in local languages their own songs, poems and prayers. The Bengali saint Chaitanya was renowned for chanting and dancing in public. He popularized the following mantra:

> *Hare Krishna, Hare Krishna,*
> *Krishna Krishna, Hare Hare,*
> *Hare Rama, Hare Rama,*
> *Rama Rama, Hare Hare.*

On the other side of India, Mirabai, a Rajasthani princess, became renowned for her devotion to Krishna, despite persecution from her family. She finally abandoned palace life to become a wandering saint. Her religious love poems are still recited today. They express intense feelings of separation from God, a mood shared by many *bhakti* saints.

The birth of the Sikh religion

Guru Nanak (1469–1539), the founder of the Sikh religion, was influenced by the northern *bhakti* tradition. He taught the importance of chanting God's holy names, the equality of all people and the importance of *seva* (service to others). Nanak's new faith was at first closely connected to Hinduism. Only later on did it become a separate religion. Sikhism also took on a military aspect, as its members fought against the Mughals, and later the British.

A POEM BY MIRABAI

As the whole world sleeps, dear love,
I keep watch, parted from you.
In a palace of pleasure,
I sit alone and awake,
And see a forsaken girl,
with a garland of tears around her neck,
passing the night, counting stars,
counting the hours to happiness.
If I had known
that falling in love
was to fall in with pain,
I would have beaten a drum,
proclaiming far and wide
that love was banned for all!

CHAPTER 5:
BRITISH RULE IN INDIA
(1757–1947)

In 1498, Vasco da Gama became the first European to set foot in India, at Calicut on the west coast. Subsequently, in 1510, the Portuguese conquered Goa. The splendour and wealth of the Mughal Empire also attracted the interest of French, Dutch and British traders. In 1610, the British East India Company established a base in Surat and further posts in Madras (1639), Bombay (1668) and Calcutta (1690). The administrators of the company signed trade agreements with the Mughals and recruited local men for their own military force. As the East India Company expanded its influence, tensions arose between the company and both local and central rulers, which led to conflict. Robert Clive's victory at the Battle of Plassey (1757) in Bengal, heralded the end of the Mughal Empire. By 1769, the East India Company had almost complete control of European trade in India.

In 1857, rumour spread among Indian soldiers that their rifle bullets were greased with the fat of cows and pigs, suggesting insensitivity to both Hindu and Muslim beliefs. (Hindus believe the cow to be sacred, and Muslims consider pork and other products from the pig to be unclean.) The army rebelled in what has been called the Indian Mutiny, prompting the British government to take full control of India in 1858.

Indian troops on the side of Robert Clive during his victory over the ruler of Bengal at Plassey in 1757.

A map of India in 1857, at the time of the Indian Mutiny, also called the First War of Independence.

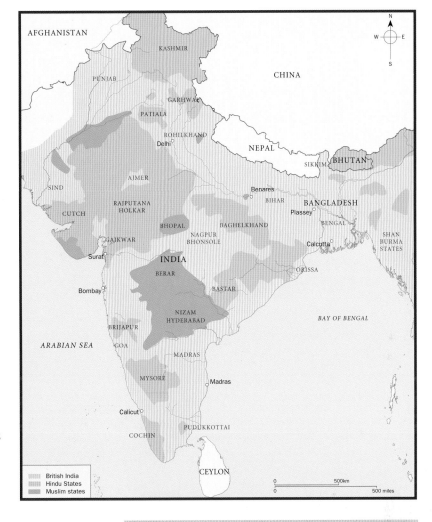

Reform movements

The early colonialists gave Hindus free rein in their religious practice. Later on, some missionaries, scholars and government officials deliberately attempted to convert Hindus to Christianity, and 'civilize' them, particularly through education. These attempts, and the growing contact between Hinduism and the West, spawned various Hindu 'reform movements'.

One of the most influential was the Brahmo Sabha, founded in 1828 by Ram Mohan Roy, and later renamed the Brahmo Samaj. Strongly influenced by Christianity, Rama Mohan disagreed with reincarnation and opposed caste practices and image worship. Today, the Brahmo Samaj continues, but with a relatively small membership.

The Arya Samaj was founded in 1875 by Swami Dayananda, who wished to halt the Christian onslaught and return to the ancient, Vedic religion. The Arya Samaj opposed what it considered later additions to Hinduism, such as image worship, ritual bathing and pilgrimage. Today, the main form of worship of the Arya Samaj is the ancient fire ceremony.

These reform movements had relatively little effect on Hindu practices, and the main traditions continued to predominate. The reform movements did succeed, however, in making Hindus more aware of their own identity as a separate religion. They also gave rise to nationalist movements, which tried to rid India of foreign rule. British rule also resulted in the emigration of Hindus to other parts of the Empire.

THE COW IN HINDUISM

The Indian Mutiny started largely through insensitivity to Hindu and Muslim beliefs. Hindu recruits objected that their bullets were greased with lard derived from slaughtered cattle. For Hindus, the cow, who so freely gives milk, is considered just like one's mother. The bull was traditionally used to plough the fields, and is therefore also accorded a high status. For these reasons, the cow and bull are special to Hindus, and offered respect. Since many Hindus are vegetarian, milk and milk products are considered helpful for a healthy diet. Ghee (clarified butter) is also important, used in cooking, for lamps and in rituals, like the ancient *havan* (fire sacrifice).

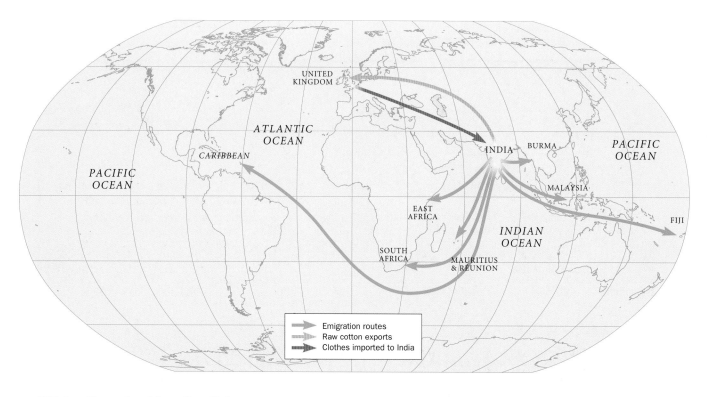

Emigration routes
Raw cotton exports
Clothes imported to India

Migration to the Caribbean

Emigration from India had been a continuous process since pre-colonial times, mainly for reasons of trade. During the colonial period, emigration to the British, French and Dutch colonies was a means of finding work. By the end of the 19th century, emigrants from India numbered almost 1.6 million.

In Britain's Caribbean colonies, the abolition of slavery (from 1834 onwards) resulted in a shortage of manpower. Western workers were reluctant to move there because they were unused to the tropical climate. Looking for other sources of labour, the colonial governments turned to the 250 million inhabitants of India.

Beginning in the 1840s, indentured labourers (workers bound by a contract) – mostly Hindi-speakers from north India – were transplanted to the British Caribbean. They were promised fair wages and return tickets in exchange for agreeing to work for a set number of years. Due to poverty, dishonest contracts from employers, and aspirations to build a new life, very few returned to India. The first Indians to arrive became labourers for the sugar industry in Trinidad. Others sailed to French Guyana and Dutch Suriname to work on the rubber and sugar plantations.

A map showing Hindu migration from around 1840 until the early 1900s.

South-East Asia and Africa

The British took formal control of the Western States of Malay in 1870. Many Tamils (from Tamil Nadu in south India) subsequently moved there to become manual labourers for the tin mines, railways and rubber plantations. Many also moved to Singapore and Burma (present-day Myanmar). From 1879, others sailed east to Fiji to work on sugar and cotton plantations. By the early 20th century, Indians constituted at least half of the population of Fiji.

Indians, many of them Hindus, also migrated to the island of Mauritius, off the east coast of Africa, and to the nearby French island of Réunion. Others, largely from Gujarat, migrated to East Africa. Many other Hindus sailed to South Africa to work on the railways and in the gold mines. It was in South Africa that Mohandas K. Gandhi – perhaps the most famous modern Hindu – worked as a lawyer. He was alarmed at colonial exploitation and the way Indians were treated as second-class citizens.

MIGRATION AND HINDU CULTURE

Emigration affected Hindu practice, as emigrants adopted cultural habits from their host communities. Hindus abroad – men especially – often began to wear Western clothes. They changed eating habits, sometimes abandoning traditional, and often vegetarian, diets. However, in some instances, Hindus living outside India became more serious about passing on their religion and culture to future generations. As with all religions, it was a struggle to maintain tradition, while at the same time adjusting to new situations.

Indian nationalism Gandhi objected to how raw Indian cotton was sent to Manchester in the UK and the clothes were then imported back into India at inflated prices. He personally boycotted cloth milled in Western factories. His struggle for fair trade was part of a growing nationalist movement calling for an end to British rule and to colonial exploitation.

A Hindu wedding in Trinidad and Tobago. The bride wears the traditional red and gold *saree*, and the groom is in white silk with a decorative turban.

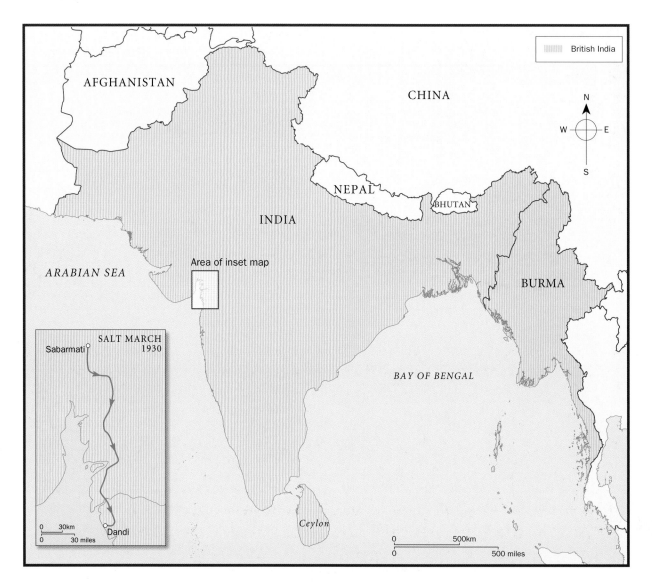

A map showing the greatest extent of India under British rule (1945). The inset map shows Gandhi's route during the salt march of 1930, a key event in the Quit India movement.

Discontent with British rule, and the resultant reform movements, gave rise to various nationalist organisations. These paved the way for India's independence, as well as its tragic partition. Since independence, nationalist sentiment has continued to play a significant role in the ongoing development of Hinduism.

Hindutva In 1909, leading members of the Arya Samaj founded the Hindu Mahasabha (the Great Hindu Assembly) to give Hindus a distinct political voice. The Mahasabha declared 'Hindustan' (India) to be 'the land of the Hindus' and demanded government according to Hindu law. In 1923, Vir Savarkar, leader of the

Mahasabha, coined the term *Hindutva*. It has been translated as 'Hinduness'. It now largely refers to organizations that advocate Hindu nationalism. These movements include the Rashtriya Swayamsevak Sangh (RSS), established in 1925, and now perhaps the most powerful Hindu organization with around five million members worldwide.

Gandhi's movement Moves towards independence increased tensions between Hindus and Muslims. For the minority Muslim community, the prospect of a Hindu government seemed little better than British rule. In 1915, Gandhi stepped onto the

HINDU VALUES

Gandhi was an avid reader of the Bhagavad Gita, which lists many desirable human values, such as:

- Non-violence to all (*ahimsa*)
- Respect for all living beings
- Humility
- Mind and sense control
- Detachment from possessions
- Service (*seva*) to God and to others
- Sustainability (*sattva*)
- Cleanliness and truthfulness

According to the Bhagavad Gita, without such values, individuals and societies cannot be peaceful or happy. Gandhi emphasized non-violence, based on the belief in the soul's presence in all life forms. For this same reason, many Hindus practise vegetarianism.

political stage, calling for unity between the two groups. Gandhi led by example. He and many of his followers wore only homespun cotton, intent on undermining the British textile industry, based in Manchester. In 1930, he organized a 384-kilometre march to the sea, where demonstrators illegally made their own salt, protesting against the British salt tax. In all these endeavours, Gandhi insisted on non-violent 'passive resistance', even in the face of aggression.

Gandhi and caste Gandhi drew much of his strength and conviction from the Hindu teachings. However, like the *bhakti* saints before him, he objected to the hereditary caste system. By his time, some people has been labelled as 'outcasts' or 'untouchables', indicating a status even lower than the fourth *varna*, the *shudras* (workers). Untouchables were allocated only the lowliest jobs, such as street cleaning or working with leather. They were often banned from eating with others, entering temples and drawing water from village wells. Gandhi renamed the untouchables Harijans, 'the children of God'.

For practical purposes, Gandhi believed in the system of four *varnas*, but not in the hereditary system, which denied equal opportunity. He wanted to incorporate the Harijans within the fourth class, the *shudra varna*. Another reformer, Ramji Ambedkar, disagreed with Gandhi on the future status of untouchables and advocated instead a completely classless society. Ambedkar later converted to Buddhism and became a hero figure for the Harijans, who renamed themselves the Dalits (the oppressed). Their struggle for equal rights continues to this day.

Mahatma Gandhi photographed during the salt march in which he personally walked the 384-kilometre route.

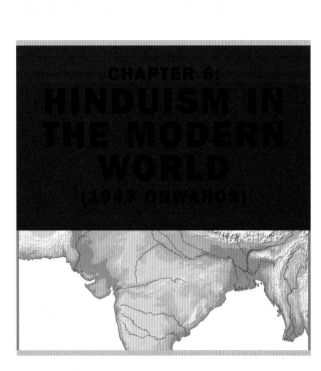

CHAPTER 6:
HINDUISM IN THE MODERN WORLD
(1947 ONWARDS)

Hindus bathe in the sacred waters of the Ganges at Varanasi during a religious festival.

Gandhi led the initial negotiations for independence, which continued in earnest after World War II (1939–1945). In 1946, Muhammed Jinnah, head of the Muslim League, conveyed the message that, for his community, an undivided India was no longer possible, as Muslims were not prepared to live under a Hindu government.

Partition Eventual independence from British rule on 15 August 1947 was therefore accompanied by the creation of the new state of Pakistan, comprised of two Muslim-majority areas in the eastern and western parts of India. Partition was accompanied by unprecedented horrors. Around half a million people were killed as no fewer than 11 million refugees – Hindus, Muslims, and Sikhs – crossed the newly drawn borders. To this day, it remains the largest recorded episode of human migration. Gandhi, greatly disappointed by partition and the ensuing violence, was assassinated in 1948 by a Hindu fanatic. His former ally, Jawaharlal Nehru, was sworn in as India's first prime minister.

Bangladesh East and West Pakistan remained one country divided by 1,600 kilometres of foreign territory, and by a gulf of cultural and linguistic differences. Feeling neglected by the government in West Pakistan, the eastern state declared independence in 1971, calling the new country Bangladesh. In the following war of independence, Bangladesh was backed by India. There were reports of further mass slaughter, particularly of Bangladeshi students and intellectuals. Bangladesh emerged victorious, and in 1979 was fully recognized as a new country.

Kashmir After partition, India forcibly assimilated smaller territories such as Hyderabad, French India and, after some time, Portuguese Goa. Kashmir, then an independent state, chose to join India, despite having a Muslim majority. Pakistan objected, leading to the first Indo-Pakistan War (1948). A stalemate resulted in a ceasefire and, finally, the assimilation of Kashmir into India. Religious and political violence continues to this day, spoiling the prospects for a region once famed for its natural beauty and rich cultural heritage.

Nepal Although India and Pakistan divided on religious lines, the new Indian state was secular, meaning that it was neutral in matters of religion. After partition, the only remaining Hindu country in the world was Nepal, lying to the north of India and south of China. Nepal was declared an independent country in 1923. Today, many Hindus of Nepalese origin also live in the Himalayan kingdom of Bhutan, making up 25 percent of its population.

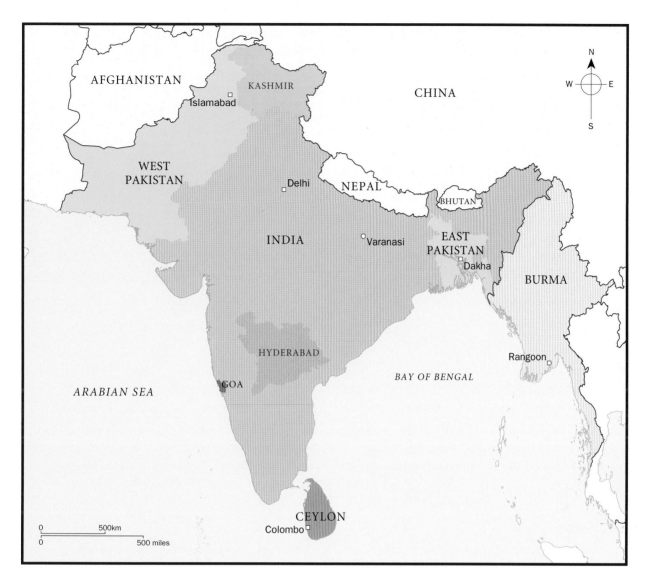

A map showing India and surrounding countries shortly after partition, including some areas of contention. More recently, ideas of 'sacred land' have been used to promote Hindu nationalism.

SACRED LAND

Whilst on pilgrimage, Hindus visit what they consider sacred land – sites connected to the lives of saints and the various deities. They take *darshan* (audience) of the local *murtis*, accept hardships (such as walking barefoot) and give to charity. A holy town is called a *tirtha*, meaning 'ford' – a place to cross over to the opposite shore (the spiritual world).

The idea of 'sacred land' has been used for political purposes. Some Hindus argue that the land of India is sacred to Hindus, and therefore India should be governed as a Hindu nation. Others claim that the Indian peninsula is special simply because it is a spiritual place, and it should not belong to any one faith. The precise relationship between India and Hinduism is debatable, especially now that increasing numbers of Hindus were born and raised elsewhere, or come from non-Indian families.

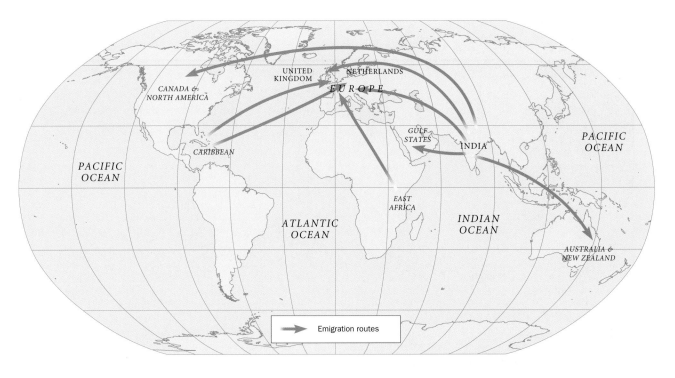

Hindu migration patterns in the latter half of the 20th century, after Indian independence.

Migration from East Africa
Indian independence heralded the rapid dissolution of the British Empire. In pursuit of India's example, many other colonies sought and achieved independence, especially between the late 1940s and the mid-1960s.

In rapid succession, the East African countries achieved self-rule: Uganda in 1962, Kenya in 1963 and the newly formed Tanzania in 1964. Through a process known as Africanization, wealth and position were returned to Africans. Many foreigners, feeling no longer welcome, decided to leave. In 1972, Hindus and other Indians were expelled from Uganda, leaving behind considerable wealth. Holding British passports, most settled in the United Kingdom, within the inner cities. Many became took on low-paid jobs or started small businesses as grocers, newsagents and clothing manufactures. The natural centres of the new Hindu communities were the first simple temples, often converted from old buildings such as church halls. Here, Hindus practised their *puja*, celebrated their festivals and performed rites of passage, such as birth ceremonies, initiations and weddings.

Largely poor at first, the British Hindu community gradually established itself socially and economically.

By the end of 20th century, Hindus excelled in education and in professional fields. Many magnificent purpose-built temples replaced the converted church halls, testifying to the growing prestige and influence of the Hindu community.

Migration from India
During the second half of the 20th century, many Hindus emigrated directly from India. Great numbers moved to North America, especially the USA, where the community now comprises almost 1.5 million. Unlike British Hindus, many of these emigrants were professionals, including doctors, engineers and IT specialists, who sought a more comfortable lifestyle. Other Indians moved to Europe, often from south India and Sri Lanka, establishing the presence of the previously under-represented south Indian Hindu traditions.

Since 1965, many Hindus have sought economic advantage in the oil-rich Arab States around the Persian Gulf. About one million now live there, mainly in Bahrain, Kuwait, Yemen, Saudi Arabia and the United Arab Emirates. They often support families in India, where the money sent home is worth far more, due to the relatively low cost of living there.

Girls dressed as Krishna (left) and his consort, Radha, at the annual Rathayatra cart festival in London. Originally celebrated in Puri, on India's east coast, the festival is now replicated in cities throughout the world.

CELEBRATING SPECIAL OCCASIONS

Commemorating special occasions is one way that Hindus maintain and pass on their traditions to the younger generation. Hindus living outside of India continue to celebrate the main festivals (see page 45) and to observe up to 16 *samskaras* (rites of passage). The most important are the birth ceremonies, the sacred-thread initiation, the wedding and the funeral. Each *samskara* marks a special event in the journey of life. Since ancient times, Hindus have divided human life into four distinct stages, called *ashrams*, as follows:

    1 *Brahmachari ashrama* – student life

    2 *Grihastha ashrama* – married life

    3 *Vanaprastha ashrama* – retired life

    4 *Sannyasa ashrama* – renounced life

Even today, a few Hindu men leave home to become *sannyasis* (monks). Some *sannyasis* travel abroad to train priests how to conduct special ceremonies and to teach Hindus how to practise their religion outside of India, within another culture.

Worldwide leaders and movements

Swami Vivekananda was a *sannyasi* and the first important Hindu to represent Hinduism to the West. In 1893, he won a standing ovation at the first World Parliament of Religions in Chicago, USA. During the post-independence emigration, many other gurus travelled west to help the growing Hindu communities. Some started their own movements, often attracting Western followers.

The hippie movement of the 1960s, with its shunning of social conventions and pursuit of a more spiritual way of life, drew much of its inspiration from India. Yoga and meditation became fashionable. The Transcendental Meditation movement, led by a guru called the Maharishi, attracted the interest of celebrities such as the Beatles. Alternative religions, often of Eastern origin, appealed to many young people. Popular religious groups included the Divine Life Society (founded by Swami Shivananda), the Divine Light Mission (now called Elan Vital) and followers of the late and controversial guru, Rajneesh (now called Osho). One of the most noticeable was the Hare Krishna movement, whose male members shaved their heads, wore traditional saffron robes and chanted and danced on the streets of cities throughout the world.

Since the 1960s and 1970s, other Hindu groups have gained popularity. These include the Swaminarayan Movement from Gujarat, which in 1995 opened an impressive, traditional stone temple near London. The Himalayan Academy is a south Indian Shaiva tradition, known for its glossy magazine entitled *Hinduism Today*. More recently, a guru called Ravi Shankara and his Art of Living Foundation have become influential.

Some groups and their leaders do not use the term Hinduism. They consider the term, originally given by outsiders, to be sectarian (stressing the differences between the various religious traditions). These include Satya Sai Baba, who claims to be an incarnation of both Shiva and Shakti, and the Brahma Kumaris, whose members are mainly women.

Women gurus

Traditionally, women in Hinduism are expected to

Members of the Hare Krishna movement chanting and dancing in Boston, USA, during the late 1960s.

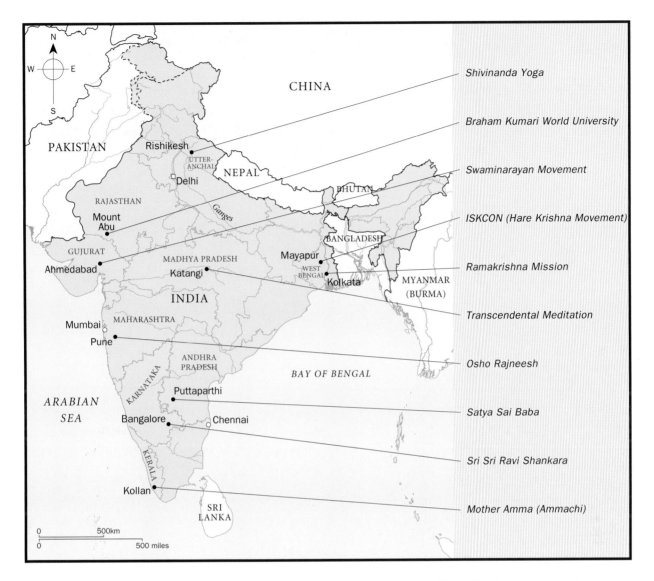

A map showing the Indian headquarters of some of the most important worldwide Hindu movements today.

marry and faithfully serve their husbands. Despite this, there are many examples of powerful and assertive Hindu women. Some, such as Sita (Rama's wife), strictly followed Hindu custom regarding dealings between men and women. Others, such as Mirabai, defied convention in the name of spiritual equality. Some traditions, though not all, have accepted women as gurus. Today, there are number of women gurus, such as Ammachi, Nirmila Devi and Mother Meera.

HINDU CULTURE

Indian and Hindu culture are visible throughout the world. For example, many Indian words – such as *chutney, pyjamas* and *bungalow* – entered the English language at the time of the British Empire. More recently, India's spiritual influence has become apparent through the arrival of terms such as *guru, karma* and *avatar*.

Hindu and Indian culture have also had a big impact on Western lifestyles, with the continuing interest in yoga and meditation; complementary health treatments, such as Indian Ayurvedic remedies; home accessories, such as incense; fashion items, like nose studs; and Indian cuisine and restaurants.

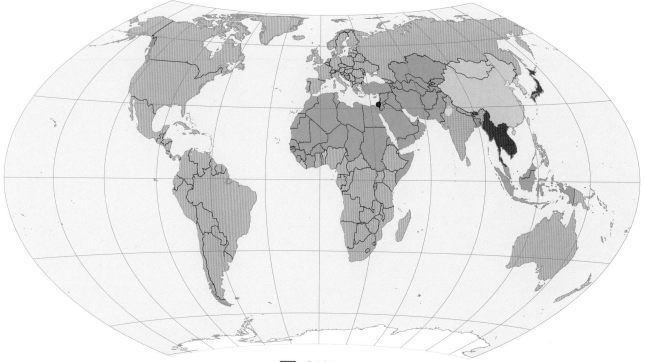

Buddhism
Christianity
Hinduism
Indigenous Religions
Islam
Judaism
Non-religious
Sikhism

A map showing the location of the majority of Hindus, compared to people of other world faiths.

Hinduism and Indian politics

India's first Prime Minister, Jawaharlal Nehru, was succeeded by Lal Shastri, and shortly after by Nehru's daughter, Indira Gandhi. In 1984, during her second term of office, Sikhs lobbied for their own state in the Punjab, and militants locked themselves in the most sacred Sikh temple, the Golden Temple in Amritsar. Government troops stormed the complex, infuriating the Sikh community. Indira Gandhi was subsequently assassinated by Sikh members of her personal guard. The ensuing violence further strained the previously amicable relationship between Sikhs and Hindus.

Tension also continued between Hindus and Muslims. In 1992, Hindu militants destroyed the Babri Mosque in Ayodhya, apparently on the site of Rama's birthplace.

Hindu Identity

For Hindus in India and abroad, interaction with other cultures has raised questions about their identity. The very idea of Hinduism as a single religion, comparable to other major faiths, is relatively new. Researchers say that the word *Hinduism* was only coined in the 19th century. Hindu nationalists suggest otherwise, emphasizing that Hinduism is an Indian religion and that India should be a Hindu country. Other Hindu thinkers stress that the universal teachings of Hinduism extend well beyond India.

In attempting to relate their ancient teachings to modern life, Hindus are faced with other vital questions. Is the idea of four *varnas*

relevant to life today? In Hindu society, should women now play an identical role to men? Can Hindus embrace modern science and medicine while remaining true to their faith?

Hinduism as a Spiritual Path

For many Hindus, their tradition is primarily a source of spiritual inspiration. They value worship and meditation as a means towards self-improvement and building a better world.

Many Hindus have been inspired by their religious convictions to take part in environmental projects. They believe in global *karma* (reaping the results of past actions), the unity of all creatures (as the *atman* is present in all species of life), and freedom from greed. Such principles have prompted them to help protect and conserve the planet.

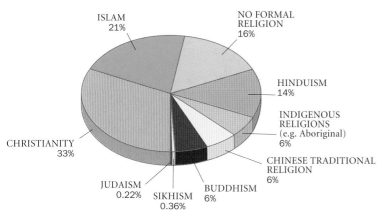

ISLAM
21%

NO FORMAL
RELIGION
16%

HINDUISM
14%

INDIGENOUS
RELIGIONS
(e.g. Aboriginal)
6%

CHINESE TRADITIONAL
RELIGION
6%

CHRISTIANITY
33%

JUDAISM
0.22%

SIKHISM
0.36%

BUDDHISM
6%

Above: This pie chart shows the size of the world's Hindu population compared to other faiths.

Below: Indian Hindus offer special prayers for world peace in Mumbai in May 2004. More than 15,000 Hindus recited mantras while throwing unbroken grains into a sacred fire.

Most Hindus also disagree with the proposition that any one faith is the only true faith, and stand firmly against intolerance and religious violence. They consider that God is the same for all people, despite their different belief systems.

Towards a Peaceful World

Hinduism prides itself on being a peaceful religion. It teaches that without inner peace we cannot be happy, no matter how much we try to adjust the world around us. Hinduism itself faces many challenges in trying to adapt its ancient teachings to a rapidly changing world. Yet it remains a vibrant, colourful and evolving tradition. Its ancient values, based on service to others and the spiritual equality of all creatures, can make a positive contribution to the 21st century.

PRAYER FOR WORLD PEACE

May good fortune pervade the entire universe, and may all envious people be pacified. May all living beings become contented by practising bhakti-yoga, *for by accepting devotional service they will think of each other's welfare. Therefore, let us all engage in the service of the one Supreme Lord.*

Bhagavat Purana 5.18.9.

GREAT LIVES AND LEGENDARY FIGURES

Krishna

Krishna is one of the principal Hindu deities. Tradition states that he was born in about 3000 BCE in the ancient city of Mathura, and raised in the nearby village of Vrindavana. He is most famous for his childhood mischief and his amorous affairs with the young cowherd girls (*gopis*). As an adult, he became the powerful king of Dwaraka and he spoke the Bhagavad Gita, later written down and now one of the most important Hindu texts. His departure from Earth marked the beginning of the present Kali yuga (age of iron). *Kali* literally means 'quarrel'.

Yudhisthira

A contemporary of Krishna, Yudhisthira was one of the five Pandavas (sons of Pandu). He became renowned as a virtuous and selfless leader. He and his brothers were persecuted by their wicked cousins (the Kauravas) and spent 13 years in exile. After the Battle of Kurukshetra, Yudhisthira was crowned emperor. At the onset of the Kali yuga, Yudhisthira renounced the throne and retired to the Himalayas.

Draupadi

A central figure in the Mahabharata, Draupadi became the common wife of all five Pandavas. Yudhisthira lost her in a rigged gambling match, and the Kauravas tried to disrobe her before the entire royal assembly. The kings present failed to intervene and sowed the seeds of their destruction on the plains of Kurukshetra. Draupadi's story illustrates the ideal of valuing and protecting women, and the consequences of neglecting or exploiting them.

Andal (725–755 CE)

Andal was the only woman among the south Indian Alvars (poet-saints). A childless couple found her under a sacred Tulasi bush and gave her the name Kothai (born of the earth). As a child, she set her mind on marrying Vishnu. According to tradition, she merged into the deity of Vishnu after being formally married to him. Her hymns are still recited in south India, where many shrines remain dedicated to her.

Shankara (780–812)

Shankara was the first of several key Hindu philosophers (including Abhinavagupta, Ramanuja and Madhva). Aged eight, he formally renounced worldly life and travelled widely, debating with Buddhists and other members of the non-orthodox movements. He thus re-established the importance of the Hindu holy books. Shankara founded the advaita school of Vedanta philosophy and is therefore addressed as Shankaracharya (the suffix *acharya* means 'great teacher'). He is often called Adi Shankara (the original Shankara) to differentiate him from the later leaders who, to this day, are also called the Shankaracharya.

Chaitanya (1486–1534)

A great logician in his youth, Chaitanya later taught that *bhakti* (devotion) is the path of true wisdom. He became a *sannyasi* (a person who renounces worldly life) at 24 and was highly regarded for his spirituality. He inspired Bengali Vaishnavism, whose followers express devotion through singing and dancing. Chaitanya was later considered a dual avatar (incarnation) of Krishna and his consort, Radha. His influence still extends through the Hare Krishna movement.

Mirabai (1547–1614)

Mirabai is perhaps the most famous female saint within Hinduism. She was a Rajasthani princess who considered Krishna her true love. She married the king of Chitor, whose family could not tolerate Mirabai's devotion to Krishna, and consequently persecuted her. She finally abandoned family life to travel and sing the glories of her chosen lord. Her songs and poems are still popular among Hindus, particularly throughout northern India.

Lakshmi Bai (c. 1830–1858)

Lakshmi Bai was born in Varanasi within a royal family. Her childhood name was Manikarnika. Later, she married the king of Jhansi. After her husband's untimely death, the British refused to accept the couple's adopted son as their legitimate heir and attempted to take over the kingdom. Lakshmi Bai fought valiantly during the Indian Mutiny (or the War of Independence, as many Hindus call it). She was killed in 1858 during the siege of Gwalior.

Vivekananda (1863–1902)

Vivekananda was born into a wealthy Bengali family and became the favourite disciple of the famous mystic Ramakrishna. Vivekananda studied Shankara's Vedanta philosophy and impressed the Western world through his presentation to the World Parliament of Religions in Chicago (1893). He travelled extensively, promoting reform and modernization of Hindu thought and practice. He established the Ramakrishna Mission, still influential through its social and educational programmes.

Mohandas Gandhi (1869–1947)

Gandhi is probably the best-known Indian of the twentieth century. He tried to free his country from British rule, and unhealthy economic dependence on Britain, through *satyagraha* (grasping the truth), *ahimsa* (non-violence) and an unswerving faith in God. He followed many orthodox practices and was particularly fond of the Bhagavad Gita. He is most well known for his support of the untouchables. He died at the hands of an assassin, disappointed with the partition of his beloved India.

FURTHER INFORMATION

Books

The Hindu Experience by Liz Aylett and Kevin O'Donnell (Hodder and Stoughton, 2000)
Hindu Prayer and Worship by Anita Ganeri and Rasamandala Das (Franklin Watts, 2006)
Twenty-first Century Religions: Hinduism by Rasamandala Das (Hodder Wayland, 2005)
Hindu Festivals Through the Year by Anita Ganeri (Franklin Watts, 2003)

Websites

www.btinternet.com/~vivekananda/schools.htm
A relatively simple site written especially for school children

hinduism.iskcon.com/index.htm
A more detailed site designed specifically for educational purposes.

www.bbc.co.uk/schools/gcsebitesize/hotlinks/re.shtml
An informative site with useful links.

DVD

Gandhi (1982)
Educational as well as entertaining, this film gives insights into the life and character of Mohandas Gandhi.

TIMELINE

c.3000   According to Hindu tradition, Krishna appeared on Earth and spoke the Bhagavad Gita (Song of God). The beginning of Kali yuga (age of iron).

c.2500   Great cities of Indus and Sarasvati valleys at the height of their power.

c.1500   The Aryans possibly invade India, bringing the beginnings of Hinduism.

c.1500–500   The Vedas are composed in the ancient language of Sanskrit. The focus is on the sacred fire ceremony (*havan*) and reaching the ancestors in heaven. The main deities, headed by Indra (god of rain), represent the forces of nature.

c. 500 BCE–500 CE   Buddhism and Jainism spread throughout India. Amongst Hindus, temple *puja* (worship of the *murti*) becomes popular, and Vishnu, Shiva and Shakti emerge as the main deities. The Epics and the Puranas are written. The Mauryan Empire (321–184 BCE) unites much of India, and the reign of the Guptas (320–550 CE) is a golden age for Hindu arts. Hinduism becomes established in South-East Asia.

500–1000   Poet-saints of south India compose many devotional poems.

800–1300   Great *acharyas* (teachers) establish branches of philosophy and corresponding *sampradayas* (succession of teachers and disciples). Shankara (c. 780–812) teaches an impersonal concept of God and re-establishes the importance of Hindu texts. Buddhism declines in India. Abhinavagupta (c. 975–1025) lays the foundation for Kashmiri Shaivism, and Ramanuja (1017–1137) advocates that God is ultimately personal.

1200–1500   Muslims rule in the north, where the Delhi Sultanate is established (1206). Hindu kingdoms, especially of the Chola dynasty, flourish in the south with Shaivism as the main tradition.

1200–1700   Many devotional saints, such as Chaitanya, Mirabai, Vallabha and Tukarama, live during this period. Guru Nanak (1486–1538) establishes the Sikh religion.

1526   The Mughal Empire is founded in India.

1600s–1700s   Many Europeans arrive in India for trade purposes.

1757   After the Battle of Plassey, India comes under British domination.

1828   The Brahmo Samaj is founded, one of many organizations seeking to reform Hinduism, largely in response to European influences.

1830 onwards   Many Hindus migrate to Fiji, Malaysia, Mauritius, the Caribbean, East Africa and South Africa.

1858   India is officially assimilated into the British Empire.

1869   The birth of Mahatma Gandhi, who later leads the struggle for Indian independence.

1947   India gains independence but loses territory, especially to the newly created Pakistan.

1950s–1970s   Many Hindus migrate to North America (from India), to the UK (from East Africa and India) and to other countries, such as Holland and Australia.

1960s   Indian thought and practices, such as yoga, become popular in the West, with groups like Transcendental Meditation and the Hare Krishna movement.

1990 onwards   Hindu communities become more established in the West, constructing many large temples.

FACTS AND FIGURES

Hindu Festivals and Holy Days

Month	Event	What happens
January/February	Sarasvati Puja	First day of spring and worship of Sarasvati
February/March	Maha Shiva Ratri	Birthday of Shiva
March	Holi	Spring festival with throwing of coloured powders
March/April	Rama Navami	Rama's birthday
April	Hanuman Jayanti	Hanuman's birthday
August	Raksha Bandana	Celebrates the love between brother and sister
August/September	Janmashtami	Krishna's birthday
August/September	Ganesh Chaturthi	Ganesh's birthday (especially popular in Mumbai)
September/October	Navaratri/Durga Puja	Worship of the goddess Devi over nine nights
October/November	Diwali	New Year worship of Lakshmi, goddess of wealth

Approximate numbers of Hindus worldwide

Year	Number
1900	215,000,000
1950	320,000,000
2005	950,000,000

Approximate numbers of Hindus in different regions of the world

Region	Number	Region	Number
Australia, New Zealand and Fiji	410,000	Malaysia	1,510,000
Bangladesh	14,430,000	Mauritius	615,000
Bhutan	558,000	Pakistan	3,280,000
Canada	330,000	Persian Gulf States	1,000,000
Caribbean	245,000	Netherlands	165,000
China	131,000	Singapore	177,000
East Africa	667,000	South Africa	530,000
Guyana	268,000	Sri Lanka	3,010,000
India	90,000,000	Suriname	118,000
Indonesia	4,380,000	USA	1,500,000
		United Kingdom	910,000

GLOSSARY

acharya Literally 'one who teaches by example'; a title applied to some great Hindu scholars.

ahimsa Non-violence towards all creatures; a value taught by Mohandas Gandhi.

arti A ceremony in which a lamp, incense and flowers are offered to sacred images.

Aryans Literally 'noble people'. Some scholars claim that the Aryans were a distinct race who invaded India and started Hinduism.

ashrama A stage of life; for Hindus there are four successive *ashramas* (see page 37).

atman The real self, or soul, which is eternal and present in all forms of life.

avatar An incarnation of a Hindu deity. The most famous are the ten avatars of Vishnu.

Bhagavad Gita 'The Song of God'; perhaps the most popular Hindu holy book.

bhajan Literally 'worship'; it specifically refers to a holy song.

bhakti Devotion; *bhakti* yoga is the path of loving service to God.

Bharata An ancient term for India, after a king of the same name.

Brahman The eternal reality, or spirit, which pervades and supports everything.

brahmin A priest or scholar, a member of the highest *varna*.

caste system The social system based on four *varnas* and other sub-groups; in more recent times, the caste system has been determined by birth rather than qualification.

darshan Literally 'seeing' or 'perspective'; one of six orthodox schools.

dharma Religious duties; more specifically, 'duties that sustain us according to our nature'.

Diwali 'Row of lights', referring to the most popular Hindu festival.

Dravidians The original inhabitants of India, especially those who now live in the south.

havan The ancient fire ceremony, which is still performed at weddings and other events.

karma 'Action' or 'the results of action', as used in 'the law of *karma*'.

kirtan 'Glorification of God'; a chant set to music.

mantra A string of sacred syllables recited as a form of prayer or meditation.

moksha Liberation from *samsara*; one of the four aims of human life.

murti A sacred image, usually made of wood, stone, brass or marble.

Om The most famous mantra; it is said, Lord Brahma heard it just prior to creation.

orthodox Following the established rules of a faith.

puja Worship, especially of the sacred image. A temple priest is called a *pujari*.

Puranas Hindu holy books; they contain many stories and legends.

Ramayana The story of Rama and Sita; one of the two Hindu epics.

sampradaya An unbroken line of teachers and disciples promoting a specific philosophy.

samsara The ongoing cycle of repeated birth and death, through the process of reincarnation.

Sanatana Dharma 'The eternal religion'; another name for Hinduism.

sannyasi A wandering monk; a person in the fourth *ashrama* (stage of life).

Sanskrit An ancient language connected to Hinduism and still used for study and worship.

tirtha 'Ford'; a holy site that enables pilgrims to 'cross to the other shore' (achieve liberation).

Trimurti 'Three deities', referring to the main deities of Brahma, Vishnu and Shiva.

unorthodox Not conforming to the accepted traditional form of a particular religion.

Vaikuntha 'The place of no anxiety'; the spiritual world.

varna Social group; there are four varnas in the system, called *varnashrama*.

Veda Important Hindu holy books; there are four Vedas.

Vedanta 'Conclusion of the Vedas'; one of the six *darshans*, or orthodox schools.

Vedic Connected to the Vedas.

yajna Sacrifice, the principal method of worship during the Vedic period.

yoga A process of linking to God; there are four main ways.

INDEX